# Your Complete Forecast 2020 Horoscope

# ARIES

# Your Complete Forecast 2020 Horoscope

# ARIES

BEJAN DARUWALLA
with
NASTUR DARUWALLA

Ranvir Books
HarperCollins *Publishers* India

First published in India by
HarperCollins *Publishers* in 2019
A-75, Sector 57, Noida, Uttar Pradesh 201301, India
www.harpercollins.co.in

2 4 6 8 10 9 7 5 3 1



P-ISBN: 978-93-5357-291-4
E-ISBN: 978-93-5357-292-1



Typeset in 11.5/15 Sabon
By Saanvi Graphics, Noida

Printed and bound at
MicroPrints India, New Delhi

# Contents

# ARIES

21 March–19 April

**Symbol: The Ram**

**Ruling Planet: Mars**

**Fire-Cardinal-Positive**

**The Sign of the Pioneer, the Explorer**

**Ganesha summarizes you in the three As: Ambition, Aggression, Achievement**

In the name of Ganesha, I have used a new method specially for you. It is the philosopher's stone that represents the planet Mars. It means control of anger and unruly emotions – direct your energy towards positive action, bravely take risks, act courageously and vigorously. The planet Mars is an active force in our lives, strengthening our energy, creativity and sex drive. Mars is the god of war, whose sword indicates direct action as he stands poised above the vessel – the philosophic egg. The strike of his sword symbolizes the purifying fire that heats the vessel.

Your colour is red, your number is nine and your direction is south.

My book is mainly by Western astrology. But the mantra I give for you is from the Vedas. The mantra is '*Om Kram Kreem Krom Sa Bhowmaya Namah*'. You may recite it nine times every Tuesday. But I always say the choice is yours and I do not force people into anything.

This picture shows you all about your own planet Mars.

A picture is worth a thousand words.

## JUPITER

Jupiter will be in your tenth angle from 2 December 2019 to 18 December 2020 which means, in simple language, that you will be at the height of your powers. It means prestige, power, position, perks – the four Ps – will be yours. Responsibility in irreversible, monumental proportions will be thrust upon you, but that will give you the authority and ability to handle pressure – and that's ultimately important. Prestige does a huge pole vault; parents figure in your scheme of things, inheritance and possession will show up on the Internet of your individual life. You learn to play splendidly with all kinds of gizmos and new-fangled gadgets, and the various media of communication. The health of parents, elders and in-laws could, however, cause concern; and the same goes for your boss and superiors. Your proficiency and performance will be at an all-time high and this should give the necessary confidence to achieve your targets / goals. In practical terms, this is what astrology is all about – giving confidence. Honours, awards and rewards sum it all up nicely.

My experience of sixty-five years in astrology has convinced me that Jupiter stands for prosperity, progress, pious deeds, achievements and divine blessings.

## SATURN

In simple language, Saturn means duty, responsibility, karma and right action. Saturn is the controller who sometimes whips you for your own good. Yes, I agree, Saturn is many times the chief cause of suffering, pain and misery but to me, that is life. You may or may not agree with me. I keep an open mind.

Saturn will be also be in your tenth angle from 1 January 2018 to most of 2020. In simple language, whether you like it or not, duty, responsibility and looking after others will be thrust upon you. I repeat word for word what I said about Saturn in 2019.

Saturn in your tenth angle means power and push. But if you cross the limits, it certainly means a downfall, a big crash from a great height. I do not want you to do that. Luckily for you, in 2019, Saturn is helped by Neptune, the planet of imagination and vision. Therefore, do think of yourself. But also think of others. Let me make it very clear: In any matter that has to do with organization, industry, handling large groups of people, social work, heavy complexes and plants, new projects and ventures, you will have the ability, skill and confidence to push ahead bravely and powerfully. This could be used as a tool or a wedge to gain your ends. In short, be venturesome, be brave but also respect the desires and wishes of others. Let me put it all in a different way. Be a great commander. But also, be a fine listener. That is the secret. Rise is certain but fall remains in your own hands. Your ambition is great, your drive is tremendous. I agree to it. But try to control your ego and all will be well.

But there is one important difference. Jupiter will also be in your tenth angle along with Saturn. Therefore, it means that what you did not achieve last year, you will do it now, your suffering will be less, your power and prestige much more. Let me put it in a different way. Your opportunities and chances of happiness and joy will be much more. Most Ariens have the capacity to take the rough with the smooth. But now the smooth part will be more evident.

As Uranus has changed signs from March 2019, it will be excellent for you in 2020.

## BLUEPRINT FOR THE ENTIRE YEAR

**January:** Up and about, hard-working, you will be ready to be on the go, be it home or office.

**February:** Fun and games, friendship and fraternity, gains and gaiety.

**March:** Too many things happening all together; see that you conserve your energy/vitality.

**April:** Month of progress, prosperity, pelf and getting things done.

**May:** Loans, funds, deals, transactions, buying and selling.

**June:** Assignments, communication, transport, ties, trips, relatives.

**July:** Home, house, family, shopping, renovation, decoration, alteration.

**August:** Trips, ceremonies, rites, fame and name, future plans.

**September:** Work, health, rewards, service, pets, projects, colleagues, promotion.

**October:** Love, marriage, law cases, relationships, travel, contracts, communication, enemies.

**November:** Joint finance, loans, funds, immigration, moving, shifting, capital formation, passion, sex.

**December:** Joy, publicity, travel, ceremony, functions, parties, invitations, import and export, collaboration, contacts and happiness because of abundance.

Listen carefully, mighty Ariens, your main planet is forceful, egoistical Mars. In other words, Mars is the warrior of the entire zodiac. I am not encouraging you to go to war. But when you want to achieve your desires and complete your plans and deliver the goods as we say, I have given the time for it below, because your own planet will guide and help you. From 19 November 2019 to 2 January 2020, Mars will help you in terms of finance and romance. From 3 January to 15 February 2020 is wonderful for travel, research, freedom and opening the vistas of your mind. From 31 March to 12 May, friends, socializing and group activities give you health, wealth and happiness. This may be a cliché but it will come true. From 28 June to 6 January 2021 is possibly your period of name, fame, opportunities, recognition, awards and rewards. In other words, June onwards, you will be at your very best. Ganesha blesses you.

In one word, Aries is the ignition key to life itself.

**Your happiness quota will be 79 per cent.**

# WEEKLY REVIEW BY PHASES OF THE MOON

## 10 January: Full Moon in Cancer

The overlying theme of this week is finance and you will be busy with loans, funds, buying and selling of personal assets, even trying your luck in the stock market. It is time for new beginnings and you are keen to make your work more profitable. You will be motivated to maintain a regular fitness regime including relaxation exercises which will help you enjoy good health. There will also be harmony at home and good times with your spouse/partner and other family members. The year starts well and you can look forward to great times.

## 17 January: Moon's Last Quarter in Libra

The moon in your own sign helps you consolidate the gains of the recent past. You will be daring and enterprising, and even a pioneer of sorts. Money trends are positive as you ponder your goals and aims for the current year. Setting goals, making plans and implementing them will occupy you and keep your energy levels high. You push ahead with all guns blazing and see most of your plans being realized. There will be adventure and daring in all your interactions and you may be drawn into several affairs of the heart. Ganesha advises you not to neglect work and to be discreet in romance lest it spill over into work and the home, and lead to problems/worries.

## 24 January: New Moon in Capricorn

You have a creative streak and find ingenious solutions to your money and relationship problems. Despite it, you are plagued by a sense of insecurity deep down. It is possible that you feel restless and dissatisfied with your life and this could spill over into your intimate relationships. Children and pets could be a source of worry. Travel for work/pleasure will be beneficial; you attend meetings, seminars and conventions and win applause for your prowess in work. This is also a good time to start laying the foundation for a spiritual quest through meditation, relaxation techniques and chanting.

## 2 February: Moon's First Quarter in Taurus

This is a time to slow down but it won't be easy as your sights are firmly fixed on making more money. Children/siblings/ extended family will crave and need your attention and your time. Health may need attention too and alternative therapies will prove effective. Visits to places of worship will calm your agitated mind. You look for truth and the meaning of life, and may seek out a guru for guidance. But you have nothing to worry on the material plane as your bank balance is quite strong. Your life is fairly well balanced but there could be stagnation in relationships. A change in perspective combined with an open-minded and flexible attitude will help bring about harmony here too.

## 9 February: Full Moon in Leo

Your interest in money matters continues and you think of ways and means to increase your assets. You love making money and spending it too. You can also be flamboyant and make it a point to display your material worth. Meetings with financial planners and dealing with loans, funds, assets will keep you occupied. There will be fun times too with social outings with loved ones. This is a good period in life and you taste success in whatever you do.

## 19 February: Moon's Last Quarter in Scorpio

This financially hectic period of the past few weeks slows down and there is a sense of a quiet and calm now. This low-key period could propel you to seek out adventures and shake things up a bit. Nothing ventured, nothing gained – so true in your case, and you are ready to try your luck, gamble away your money, and also seek out adventures of the heart. You might even find the courage to propose to your sweetheart, and then there may be an engagement or marriage on the cards, Ganesha urges you to be bold and brave and to keep your wits about you to extract the most out of this phase.

### 23 February: New Moon in Aquarius

Keep your bags packed as you may have many trips this coming week. Yes, says Ganesha, be prepared to take overnight trips or short getaways for both work and pleasure. Meeting new people and even those you have lost touch with – personally or through email, phone or snail mail – is not ruled out. Check out new technology to raise your communication levels. There will be some obstacles at work but the family and close friends are behind you like a rock to motivate and support you. So don't lose heart. You manage to make progress despite the odds. Your determination and enterprise will ensure that you pull through difficult situations.

## 2 March: Moon's First Quarter in Gemini

It is definitely 'relationship time' now as the new moon phase draws your attention to those who have added value to your life. You also have the cooperation and support of your boss and co-workers. People find you pleasant and agreeable as you go out of your way to help others in need. There may be a windfall now and you could gain a lot from an inheritance which you didn't expect. Loans/interest/bonuses and even payments stuck for a long time will now be accessible to you. Don't go overboard and spend it all. Exercise control and be moderate, says Ganesha, and success is yours.

## 9 March: Full Moon in Virgo

A really busy week, even a hectic one, as everyday chores take your time. Despite leaving you totally engrossed and sometimes exhausted, it is still an enjoyable week. You also manage to find time for your spiritual aspirations. Apart from work, there are social interactions and quality time spent with friends, family and loved ones. You love entertaining and being entertained, and there will be a plethora of outings, picnics and get-togethers. You will be the soul of the party. Your emotions are more intense now and you may have to keep a tab on mood swings. There will be opposing energies at play and you will have to keep the balance. Take care of your health in this phase.

## 16 March: Moon's Last Quarter in Sagittarius

Your fine interactions with people, especially with family members/work associates have been enjoyable and even empowering.

The introspective phase gives way to more pressing, earthly concerns. The welfare and security of your loved ones is of paramount importance now and you need to take care of their needs and wants. There could be unexpected expenses as you overreach yourself to help others. Your efforts are now diverted towards building up the family assets and also your personal wealth.

## 24 March: New Moon in Aries

Your sustained hard work now bears fruit. It is payback time now and Ganesha showers you with rewards. Salary raises, promotions and perks are part of this well-deserved package, and you will have to take care that it doesn't bloat your ego further. Other money-related matters such as funds, loans, deposits, taxes, trade, agencies, legal matters could give you gains, both expected and unexpected, and could become a cause of great jubilation at home. There could be overseas travel and some medical issues to attend to. The health of an older family member may be a cause for concern.

## 1 April: Moon's First Quarter in Cancer

You love to make money and you make a lot of it quite effortlessly, as the new moon in your own sign initiates a trend of gains. Money continues to flow into your coffers through rents, leases, loans and promissory notes. A good bank balance makes you feel secure. You may have to spend a lot of time on negotiations and deals, buying/selling of assets and making acquisitions. Your life is on an upswing in this monthly trend and you work at a new image for yourself. You may go in for a makeover and change your wardrobe, hairstyle and even body image. You may take on a club membership which will help expand your social circle. You spend on yourself but isn't that also a type of investment?

## 8 April: Full Moon in Libra

It is definitely money that is in focus this week. A strong financial foundation is what you hanker after, as it gives you a feeling of security. You do this through prudent and long-term investment in land, property, assets and stock holdings. This will give you the necessary push to achieve success and, in the process, develop your identity too. Everything falls smoothly into place like the pieces of a jigsaw puzzle, almost preordained and without any great effort on your part. Ganesha seems determined to ensure that you are in the right time and so it is no surprise to see how swiftly your efforts bear fruit. But it is possible that over-involvement with work could cause you to neglect your spouse/home/kids and even your health. Fortunately, in the end, all your efforts will be rewarded.

## 14 April: Moon's Last Quarter in Capricorn

You have been working very hard these past few weeks and could have neglected your emotional relationships in the bargain. Romantic matters now come into sharp focus and you bond with your partner in a powerful way. You feel good about it and this, fortunately, infuses a feel-good factor which also colours your ties with your colleagues, co-workers, siblings and even extended family. The mood is contagious and everyone is happy. Those who are unattached can expect to find love too. A sense of joyousness permeates your being and you feel physically fit too.

## 23 April: New Moon in Taurus

Carpe diem! (Seize the day!) This is the motto that truly defines this exciting time in your life. Drink to life and savour each mouthful to the fullest, says Ganesha. You can have it all, if you want. Love, romantic relations, fun and games, partying, socializing, get-togethers – yes, all these appeal to you and fill your plate till it is overflowing. Relationships, both personal and professional, give you great pleasure and benefit you in manifold ways. You look towards the future with hope and optimism in your heart. Nothing dims your happiness and you are eager to help those less privileged than you. You find a strange satisfaction at work and this joyful spirit adds colour to your life. You couldn't have asked Ganesha for more, could you?

## 30 April: Moon's First Quarter in Leo

A whole new trend begins this week and Ganesha predicts that it will definitely be the main theme in August too. It involves the evolution of your fast-moving, impulsive nature into a calmer, more sober one in which you develop a love for humanitarian activities. No half measures here, as you go all out to share your resources with the underprivileged. You are at the forefront, making things happen at home, work and in the community. You go about getting things done, whether it is helping new people adjust to the workplace or introducing new methods of functioning. You are socially and environmentally aware and also very humane, helping orphans or even stray animals find new homes or developing new initiatives for senior citizens in your locality. You also set about developing deeper bonds with your partner. The time could be just right for you to start a family if you wish to, says Ganesha.

### 7 May: Full Moon in Scorpio

The theme of relationships is taken further this week and you focus strongly on communicating with your loved one. You do not generally enjoy going too deep into any issue but at this stage in your life, you do just that. They do say God is in the details, don't they? This is also the time to make yourself more visible, perhaps even the right time to update that résumé, says Ganesha. Networking opportunities/the tools of modern communication are aplenty and it is easy to meet new people and old friends, and even have interactions for professional gains and career growth. There could be travel, new collaborations and much professional success.

## 14 May: Moon's Last Quarter in Aquarius

Developing and maintaining relationships is the definite trend for this month, and you may have already seen strong indications of this since last week. You will continue to strengthen your professional relationships through good communication and a thoughtful attitude. Thanks to the changed perspective and your efforts, you will also see immediate rewards. You are ready to involve other people in new projects and the money starts flowing in. You are also happy to share the profits with your partners and co-workers. This certainly helps boost their morale and leads to a pleasant working environment. If you are in business, you will be eagerly looking at the many lucrative opportunities open to you. The domestic environment will also be harmonious and will reflect your success. It is a happy period by any account.

## 22 May: New Moon in Gemini

Two themes run parallel this week. On the one hand, you add to your resources through loans, funds, rent, leases, legacies and inheritances. On the other hand, as you seek an intense connection with your partner or beloved, the possibility of a strengthened emotional bond charges you with adrenaline. You are filled with passion. Last month's romantic adventures and interludes are still playing on your mind and you are eager to take them to the next level. Honey and money, love and finances, amour and pelf – yes Ariens, this phase gives you the two best reasons to be happy! But, underlying all this, quite paradoxically, will be a streak of spirituality and mysticism which draws you into esoteric practices/tantra and mantra. There are many colours on your palette to dip into.

## 30 May: Moon's First Quarter in Virgo

Fun, frolic, friendships, finances – these four Fs have demanded your fair share of attention in the past week and you have gone all out to do them justice. Now, you want to take things easy and rest a bit. There is the danger of going to the other extreme – from intense activity to absolute indolence. Other-worldly matters bubble up, urging you to search within and get the answers to esoteric questions. Visits to holy places, short trips and pilgrimages, meditation centres, religious gatherings attract you as Ganesha offers you a chance to build up your spiritual base. You could also meet a spiritual guru/

mentor to guide you in your search for the meaning of life.

## 5 June: Full Moon in Sagittarius

You can't be kept down for too long and you think your goals and targets afresh for the month to come. Life beckons and you push ahead with your characteristics forthrightness. Hard work, creativity, innovation and optimism colour your actions as you make brilliant progress. Communications, contacts, correspondence – these three Cs – are the main trend for this month, not just in your work but even in all your personal and intimate relationships. Romantic gestures/leisure activities/outings/ movies/family gatherings keep you excited and happy. Your home is your haven and you spend special moments with your spouse/partner/children/extended family. This energizes you, gives you renewed zest for living. Great times are in store for you.

## 13 June: Moon's Last Quarter in Pisces

You realize the need to organize your time and work routine as you push ahead with the goals set last week. You introduce systems, streamline procedures and increase your efficiency at the workplace. This endears you to your colleagues and subordinates. Yes, it's action time and you may find yourself tackling many projects at one go and multitasking furiously and successfully. There will be travel, expansion and growth. You will be mentally rejuvenated, will perform wonderfully at work and will have a loving relationship with spouse, children and family elders. Finances are on the upswing and you reach the pinnacles of success.

## 21 June: New Moon in Cancer

The attention you have given to relationships over the past few weeks has opened your eyes to the great value they have in your life. It is no longer enough for you to think only about yourself, your personal goals and ambitions. You have to include others in your dreams. There are high expectations from spouse/partner/older relatives/children/ colleagues and workmates, and this could stretch your time and resources. Their needs are important too and you may not have the time, energy or the money to fulfil their desires. This bothers you no end. Meditation, going for quiet walks or indulging in some other relaxing activity will be necessary to sort this situation out. Don't allow yourself to get ensnared in emotional dramas. You have to guard against such emotionally volcanic situations.

## 28 June: Moon's First Quarter in Libra

The moon in your sign makes you want to shine in the world. You aim to be the best you can in your work and in your relationships and also want to be the centre of attraction. A strong self-image and a successful persona is what you want to project, especially to those who look up to you. Money makes both personal relationships and family interactions sweeter and you enjoy domestic bliss. You are filled with contentment as you go about your work and domestic affairs.

## 5 July: Full Moon in Capricorn

You feel a strong pull to explore new facets of your personality. Till now you have focused on your work and home and have seen glimpses of complex emotional issues emerge. You have tackled the professional front efficiently (your energy and drive are legendary, no doubt about that) but now you are eager to explore the creative side of your personality. Hobbies, children, pets and intimate relations are highlighted and you feel the urge to create something new. Innovation and ingenuity are the keywords here. Art, theatre, cinema, films, writing, designing or any creative pursuit could interest and inspire you. You have developed good people-skills which will hold you in good stead in your personal as well as your professional life.

## 12 July: Moon's Last Quarter in Gemini

Ganesha rewards you with closer bonds, genuine love and romance. This fills you with a sense of peace and well-being which no amount of money or material success can buy. These relationships are your bedrock, inspiring you to take giant strides in your chosen field. At work, a new outlook – one that is caring and tolerant – will get you the cooperation and support of your workmates and this will increase the kudos coming your way. Family members provide moments of true companionship but there could be health-related issues of older relatives that would need to be tackled. Children will be a source of joy.

## 20 July: New Moon in Cancer

You switch from the relationship-rich period of the last few weeks to professional concerns. Personal associations have been supportive on the road to material success, but you now realize that renewed efforts are required to push ahead. Spouse/lover/children/parents/servants/helpers look to you for direction and you provide it. You need a balance for life to be more harmonious and must make time for family obligations too. You have a tendency to take off on a tangent which you must curb.

## 27 July: Moon's First Quarter in Virgo

This is a pleasant phase. You have delivered virtuoso performances in both the important sectors of your life – home and work. You are the toast of everyone, the blue-eyed boy/girl and also the centre of envy. Your confidence and chutzpah, combined waters and emerge victorious. But this is not all, says Ganesha.

Another trend overlaps: finances engage your attention too. Funds, loans rentals and leases, or MoUs demand your attention. You may see an overlap as professional relationships turn more personal and there is a mixing of business and pleasure. You are the key person in these dealings/negotiations and Ganesha helps you to take the right action at the right time. Relations improve as you spend quality time, not just with your beloved, but also with your children/parents/ siblings/in-laws. There are happy times to be had by all.

## 2 August: Full Moon in Aquarius

The successful pursuit of your goals requires out-of-the-box thinking and you wholeheartedly accept the challenges that confront you. Ganesha motivates you to seek greener pastures. You could be busy with funds/loans negotiations and deals, a job change or even a surge in responsibilities (should be accompanied by promotions and in privileges). You could be also looking out for collaborations, partnerships and even dealerships. As a carryover from last week, you may still find yourself restless and so you will be drawn to a quest for peace and spiritual solace. This is a week in which you can expect the unexpected. The focus will shift, as the week unfolds, to spiritual practices, meditation and other relaxation techniques which will help you tide over the bumps of this period gracefully and safely.

### 11 August: Moon's Last Quarter in Taurus

Your spiritual practices have given you fortitude and the courage of your convictions. You feel much more calm and peaceful and ready to face life's challenges with equanimity. This doesn't mean that you are lethargic and laid-back; quite the contrary really. Ganesha says that you will be full of energy and vigour, a joie de vivre, an unalloyed enthusiasm, which helps you fulfil your responsibilities at home and at work. You will do remarkably well at work and will be suitably rewarded. Meeting deadlines with superlative ease in child's pay for you.

## 19 August: New Moon in Leo

There is a repetition of last month's theme (to a lesser degree, though) as the moon is once again in Taurus. The spotlight continues to shine on you at work, thanks to your awesome performance. Relationships are on the upswing with interpersonal tensions sorted out. Your home is your haven and you enjoy warm and caring interactions with your near and dear ones. Socializing, partying and entertaining your friends and family helps you unwind. Your popularity soars and you are the darling of your friends, family, kith and kin. Curb unhealthy ego drives or you will be the target of envy.

## 25 August: Moon's First Quarter in Sagittarius

This phase kick-starts a trend of hardwork and fervent play. Dedicated efforts and large doses of luck give you success on the domestic and professional fronts. You are more organized at work and read the fine print. You are also enthusiastic, confident and filled with a new energy which ensues success. You use your resources in a prudent manner, introducing innovative and effective measures at work, revive old contacts and friendships and clear the air with those you may have had a run-in with earlier. There is also room for interesting tie-ups and romantic liaisons. You will also hit the gym or take up some form of health improvement scheme.

## 2 September: Full Moon in Pisces

The work formats put into place last week take your productivity levels to dizzy heights.

There is a lot of work but the systems are in place and so while the productivity increases, the effort doesn't. This not only makes your work easier but also gives you more time to devote to domestic affairs. You will have tender moments with your loved one as you multitask and juggle several projects effortlessly. You may have to attend out-of-town meetings, conferences, conventions for collaborations/negotiations/tie-ups. Certain unforeseen legal matters could crop up; though not serious, they could be time-consuming. It is a week of many facets and immense possibilities.

### 10 September: Moon's Last Quarter in Gemini

You need a break from the hectic activities and events of the past weeks. Stress levels are high and you need to recuperate. You look at social work and may spend time at old people's homes and other charities. You look at ways to give back to society. Those in the healthcare professions – such as nursing, psychiatry, psychotherapy, counselling, etc. – could scale new heights, perhaps even win international acclaim for their work. Almost all of you will have unusual intuition which is actually quite different from your normal leanings, but this phase makes it happen. You have made enough money and are now hankering after spiritual gains.

## 17 September: New Moon in Virgo

You internalize and intellectualize your emotions this week, which is a natural progression of the trend that started at the full moon of last month. Astrology is a logical science, says your Ganesha devotee, and you can definitely see the proof. You indulge in genuine self-evaluation and self-awareness, and life inspires you to make changes that may be against your basic nature but which help you reach your higher self. You are usually very impatient and hasty to get your work done (even guilty very often of cutting corners, isn't it?) but this phase demands accountability. Self-mastery is the key to gains in this phase. The three Cs – contacts, contracts and correspondence – are of paramount importance too, says Ganesha. You will make rapid progress on all fronts and become a much more whole and rounded personality.

## 24 September: Moon's First Quarter in Capricorn

With your restored and enhanced perception of life, you will take it easy, be relaxed, a bit laid-back too. You are happy and optimistic and take time away from work with your lover or for social outings with friends, children and parents. You find joy in building and maintaining valuable partnerships and have a gentle, loving attitude which helps foster intimate bonds. It is not all as rosy as it sounds and you could face hurdles, setbacks and delays coupled with sluggish funds and unexpected expenses. But you will continue to socialize. There will be fun and frolic in your life, which energizes you. Somehow, you don't allow trifles to bother you.

## 2 October: Full Moon in Aries

There has been a steadily increasing awareness of the importance of relationships in your life for the past few weeks. So, a further strengthening and bonding, both at work and at home, can be achieved through mutual care and respect. Strife and friction, when they occur, should be tactfully and diplomatically handled. As we all know, peaceful solutions will lead to greater growth and progress. Control your ego and allow wiser counsel to prevail. This will be particularly relevant on the home front in your dealings with your spouse/partner. At work too, supportive colleagues and co-workers will help you perform better. Planning, delegating and working as a team player could reduce work pressures and improve output. Overall, it is a fantastic week for putting down the roots for stupendous long-term success.

## 10 October: Moon's Last Quarter in Cancer

You are determined to sustain the growth you have achieved and even build further on it. This is an action-packed week as you find your hands full at work, much more than you can handle. This moon phase in your sign reinforces the focus on your priorities and values as you push forward to take advantage of the myriad possibilities that have presented themselves to you. The rewards are immediate and, buoyed, you push ahead frenetically. This could lead to a burnout, causing more harm than good. So use available resources judiciously to avoid such an eventually. Spending time in the company of small children/pets and on hobbies/leisure pursuits could energize you.

## 16 October: New Moon in Libra

The hectic work situation slows down to some extent in this phase. You are satisfied with the way your projects have turned out and now you feel relaxed enough to spend time with your loved ones. Home matters occupy your mind and you may even delve deep into the history of your family. Family trees, older relatives, extended family, visits to the ancestral home, even taking stock of ancestral property are some of the ways the current trend may manifest in your life. Some of you, says Ganesha, may be overburdened by mundane domestic chores and so an outlet in terms of a hobby, creative pursuits, shopping, learning new skills will serve as a great release.

## 23 October: Moon's First Quarter in Aquarius

You now allow yourself to become more relaxed and enjoy a 'chilled out' time, as they say, with your loved ones. Unattached Ariens could find many opportunities to spend happy, even ecstatic, moments with someone special. The married may want to renew their marriage vows or go on a second honeymoon. This intensely passionate time also affects your money angle. You do have to pay for all your indulgences and so a tab on expenses will be prudent. It may be a good idea to avoid any new undertakings at this time.

## 31 October: Full Moon in Taurus

You have worked hard to consolidate your position and now feel confident that your finances are stable. You have taken a lot of risks earlier which could have led to some degree of loss at work. You are now cautious and read the fine print carefully. There is better rapport too between you, your co-workers and boss. You could be involved in developing new contracts or more business for your company, and will be travelling on work. This receives the full support and approval of your boss/superiors. Those in the media strike a purple patch, do remarkably well, and are applauded for their efforts.

## 8 November: Moon's Last Quarter in Leo

Having all aspects of your life running smoothly like the well-oiled wheels of an engine, you feel content as acknowledgement and appreciation pour in for your brilliant performances at work. You now enjoy an enhanced stature in society, and this is very gratifying, especially if you look back at the hard work and sacrifices you have made to get there. But now there is a complete contrast, a veritable volte-face, as you move away from the absolute grind of the past weeks to the present mood of pure elation. The frenzy of achievements has dimmed and you now want to take it easy, revelling in glorious passions with your spouse/lover, partaking of luxuries and sweet moments. Romantic energies pervade all your interactions and could lead to tricky situations vis-à-vis love affairs and secret liaisons. Children and/or hobbies provide fun and frolic. Ganesha advises you to develop healthy habits to be able to ride this exciting phase safely. Try to rein in indiscretions.

## 15 November: New Moon in Scorpio

Your confidence as well as the caring side of your nature will be at an all-time high as you give and get love and affection in equal measure from your family and loved ones. The past week has given you some exceptionally special moments, heart-warming and thoroughly enjoyable, with your spouse/lover and children/parents. The temptation of going overboard and showering them with the most precious gift of all – your time – will fill you with pure joy and happiness. The intense sharing and caring are there but, at the same time, there will be a need to consider the ground realities of your financial situation. A restricted cash flow could cause dissatisfaction and unhappiness and could need extraordinary efforts to get them back on track. Neglecting domestic duties and responsibilities could be an offshoot of your extreme involvement at work but you needn't be unduly worried as your lover or spouse/partner and even family elders provide you with the necessary support and backing (both financial and emotional). The feel-good energies of this phase will give you the strength and stamina required to achieve your business/professional goals, which could have been, at a standstill due to varied reasons. This is a period in which you make enormous progress.

## 22 November: Moon's First Quarter in Pisces

Happiness and contentment come into your personal life through the blessings of Ganesha. There is closeness and warmth in all your relationships leading to greater pleasure and cheer. Your spouse/lover showers you with love and you reciprocate. It is a lucky week in which unexpected profits flow in and allow you to enjoy the fruits of your labour. There is exultation and exuberance in your life as material successes pale in front of the ecstasy of soul-stirring relationships. The euphoria that you now experience translates into radiant health.

## 30 November: Full Moon in Gemini

Professional pursuits hold your interest. You set gargantuan goals and expect to achieve them. Each and every aspect of your life is at its peak and fills you with a heightened sense of self-worth. There are monetary gains too. Your accomplishments fill with you with pride and you are on a roll, but the tendency to neglect intimate relationships, children and health issues could again cause roadblocks in your progress. You attract trust, belief and faith and are filled with the confidence that you can realize the awe-inspiring dreams within your heart.

## 8 December: Moon's Last Quarter in Virgo

You will experience true inner peace and contentment this week. You have worked hard, conscientiously and consistently, and the results have been superlative; you were absolutely deserving of the awards and rewards that came your way. Your performances at the workplace has been stellar, to say the least, but now you look at issues far removed from the workplace. You are less fiery and ambitious and are more complacent and calm in your interactions. You mentor, guide and motivate youngsters and this gives you a sense of fulfilment. As an extension of your renewed outlook, public welfare schemes concerning the underprivileged, the needy and the destitute, make you reach out and provide solace physically, emotionally and monetarily. You feel blessed, light-hearted and spiritually satisfied.

## 14 December: New Moon in Sagittarius

You will be closer to people now, enjoying the new bonds you have forged in the past few weeks. You look forward eagerly to widen your personal horizons and the scope of your interactions and relationships. All kinds of gains have come to you but now a completely different dimension of connections, communications and collaborations open up. Geographical/physical boundaries and limitations are no longer a hindrance as a fresh universe virtually opens up before you as you make full use of the latest networking tools. With your feet placed firmly on the ground, you work hard. Finances could be tight as you dream big and need huge amounts to invest. You tap loans and the market and push ahead confidently. You are filled with optimism and energy and feel you can move mountains. Nothing seems impossible in this phase.

## 21 December: Moon's First Quarter in Aries

Ganesha gives you just about everything that you wish for. But your focus will continue to remain on your work. A strong network of friends/relatives, in-laws is your lifeline as you immerse yourself completely into professional commitments. Your efforts are scintillating, sparkling and truly divine. You plumb the depths of your inner being to bring forth creations of supreme innovation, novelty and originality. This is an excellent time for those in artistic professions. You are also assailed by intensely passionate energies, concerned with the physical expressions, and enjoyments of love, and even manifesting themselves in illicit, secret affairs/romantic liaisons/behind-the-scenes deals and activities. There could be health issues which need attention and wild mood swings too. Travel, especially short trips, could be beneficial.

## 30 December: Full Moon in Cancer

Once again, as at the beginning of this year, you come face to face with one of the most important aspects of your life. Becoming financially stable has been the cornerstone of almost all your efforts. You have persisted and persevered in planning and executing financial matters with good results. You have managed to leverage not only your profile but also your organization's kitty. Awards, rewards, funds and income from varied sources have made you and your loved ones happy. You have tasted success far beyond your wildest imagination and are now not keen to rest on your laurels. You are infused with new hope and confidence and want to push ahead without stops. Bonds with children/young people/parents/ siblings provide immense joy. You look forward to 2021, especially in the areas of money/love/spirituality. Ganesha's blessings are with you.

# Ready Reckoner for All Twelve Signs

| | | | |
|---|---|---|---|
| Aries | Assertive | Mars | Energy |
| Taurus | Possessive | Venus | Sex/love/ emotion |
| Gemini | Versatile | Mercury | Five senses |
| Cancer | Sensitive | Moon | Inner realm |
| Leo | Rulership | Sun | Personality |
| Virgo | Discrimi- nation | Mercury | Five senses |
| Libra | Balance | Venus | Sex/love/ emotion |
| Scorpio | Passion | Pluto | Transform |
| Sagittarius | Free- ranging | Jupiter | Absorb |
| Capricorn | Prudence | Saturn | Self- preservation |
| Aquarius | Objectivity | Uranus | Creativity |
| Pisces | Intuitive | Neptune | Subcon- scious |

**Keyword for every sign:**

**Aries:** Courage

**Taurus:** Dependability

**Gemini:** Responsiveness

**Cancer:** Loyalty

**Leo:** Exuberance

**Virgo:** Consciousness

**Libra:** Charm

**Scorpio:** Idealism

**Sagittarius:** Optimism

**Capricorn:** Steadiness

**Aquarius:** Friendliness

**Pisces:** Compassion

I fully agree with other astrologers that there could well be other main characteristics for every sign. Nothing is final.

# The Signs and Their Elements

**Fire Symbolic Attributes:** Energy, faith, enthusiasm, spontaneity, intuition and idealism.

Aries, Leo, Sagittarius.

**Earth Symbolic Attributes:** Basic common sense, practicality, resourcefulness, management ability and skill.

Taurus, Virgo, Capricorn.

**Air Symbolic Attributes:** Rational judgement, abstract thinking, detachment, objectivity and perspective, the intellect and the world of ideas.

Gemini, Libra, Aquarius.

**Water Symbolic Attributes:** Feelings, anxieties, psychism, sensitivity, withdrawal, emotional vulnerability, in-depth perception, mysticism, the world of the intangible.

Cancer, Scorpio, Pisces.

# World Horoscope

## BY BEJAN DARUWALLA

Ganesha says these are the salient features for our world:

Less is more

Climate change

Robots

Artificial intelligence

Systematizing life itself

Performance orientation

Technology and rationality are kings

Methodology and perfection

Managing men and matters

The best way to get things done

Precision and perfection

Health, hygiene, welfare

Canned packaged spirituality, salvation

Year 2080 is the pinnacle for mankind.

The full potential and power of the brain and neurons will evolve a new world order beyond our imagination and fantasy. It could well be the new God.

## AFRICA

Ganesha says Africa is the country of the future. Why? Firstly, my gut feeling is a sort of ESP for essence of something which we know but cannot express. Secondly, by mundane Western astrology Africa comes under the sign Cancer. Many astrologers believe life began in Africa because Cancer is the great Mother of the World. Thirdly, the Tarot card no. 21 says clearly 'The upliftment of the downtrodden and the backward'. Peace on Earth. It is on the strength of this Tarot card that I predicted the success of Obama, the first Black president of America. Now this will also apply to Africa. When? The simple answer is that the next seven years will demonstrate it.

## INDIA

For India I have said again and again that Modi was born to purify and cleanse the Ganga. I am writing this piece on 8 June 2019 and the news has flashed 'Wave of 20,000 citizens to clean Sabarmati'. A grand beginning.

## ISRAEL

Mr Benjamin Netanyahu is no more the prime minister of Israel. By mundane Western astrology a huge segment for part of the Middle East comes under the sign Taurus. Uranus is right now in Taurus and has seen the end of this Israel prime minister. Next year Uranus in Taurus will be in excellent formation with Jupiter and Saturn in Capricorn, according to

Western astrology. Normally I do not go into technicalities. But it is certainly this excellent formation which will draw all the Middle East countries nearer to each other. In other words, a new era begins. On and before 31 December 2019 to July 2025 there is a strong possibility of peace or at least a mutual respect, give and take. This will obviously lead to stability for the Middle East and in a broader sense for our world. Let me put it all in one sentence. As a poet has said, 'The best is yet to be.'

## USA

America under Donald Trump will be not loved and respected by the rest of the world. A great pity, and to me a mighty tragedy. But Japan, India, Singapore will be good friends in every possible way. Surprisingly enough, I see that under the premiership of Imran Khan, the former mighty all-rounder of cricket, a glimpse of better relationship is certainly possible. As an astrologer I must be completely objective and at the same time have a vision of things to come. Our world is complex and confused. But I see more than a glimpse of hope. I see a possibility of all of us living together if not lovingly at least in a compromise and balance of relationships. Why? We are right now in the Aquarian age. Strictly speaking, Jupiter and Saturn will be in the sign of Aquarius, and that means good things in relationships and technology will pick up great speed and there will be hope as well as confidence in our heart that we are born to live together and be happy. As I have said many times, this span will be between 2021 to 2081. Lastly, for the sake of new readers of the book, I repeat what I have said in my 2019 book. Let me now reveal the secret of my predictions. We all know that we are in the Aquarian age. In the Aquarian age there will be the marriage of technology and humanity. The planets I personally take into active consideration are Jupiter, the planet of prosperity and plenty, and Saturn, the planet of duty as well as integrity. Both these planets will come together in the sign Aquarius in 2081. Therefore, intuition and common sense both dictate that it could well be the greatest year of the twenty-first century. The cynics are most welcome to say, 'Mr Daruwalla, you and many of us will not be there to verify the accuracy of this prediction.' My answer is, 'They are more than welcome to their own opinion. To each his own is the guiding principle of my life.'

I am not God. But I try to combine all the above points by astrology and not only find out about it by fusing it with the meaning, purpose and symbol of the planets but by praying to Ganesha to help me fuse it all into one single whole. Let me put it very simply. I try to see life itself steadily and see it whole. This might appear to be a contradiction. But as John Donne the poet has said, 'Contradictories meet in me. What is there left to say.'

## Our Future

Ganesha says that technology is king. The main reason for it is we are right now in the Aquarian–Uranian age. Curiosity is the main characteristic of the Aquarian age. Thanks to curiosity, we invent new things and schemes; revolutionize the entire scheme of things and invent, innovate and create a new world order. Group activities is a must for all creative pursuits in our Aquarian age.

In this new world order, we will have to live with artificial intelligence, robotic relationships and lack of human intimacy. These are times of 100 per cent surveillance and no privacy; dangerous times of machine-made assassinations, use of social media to create hysteria against a person/organization, climate change and information expressway, which the Chinese call the 'digital silk road'.

Let me explain it in simple terms. We Indians have our Kumbha Mela, the biggest gathering in the world. It means in simple language a group activity. Group activity leads to the seven Cs – connection, communication, collectivity, contacts, creativity, circulation and consciousness. The Sanskrit word '*kumbh*' actually means Aquarius in English, and the beauty of it is we are now in the Aquarian age. The additional factor is technology and science.

The million-dollar question is whether this technology will overtake us and be finally our master or will we be able to share our life with this new technology. It is said that in Japan, man actually sleep with robots. They are very comfortable with it. I admit that this is only a rumour. It may or may not be true. But it certainly indicates what we are heading for. One thing is certain. We are masters of mass destruction but not of universal happiness despite all our technology, knowledge, understanding, psychology and a powerful grip on the basics of human nature. We are now in a position to discover, analyse and cure neurological disorders. We can also prevent it by early detection of diseases. That is indeed a very major achievement.

Let me put it very simply. We have everything going for us and yet we are so miserable. Terrorists sometimes rule our lives or at least make us absolutely miserable. There are giants in all the above-mentioned fields. I am only an astrologer. Astrology simply means the right persons at the right place and at the right time. The other term of astrology is Jyotish. '*Jyot*' means light and '*Ish*' means God. Therefore, to us Indians, Jyotish is the light of God. I do not pretend to be a superman, a religious leader or a guru. I can only say that I have met three prime ministers of India, helped people in whatever way I can and now, at eighty-eight, this is what I predict in the name of my Master and Lord Guru.

## URANUS

In this Aquarian age of technology and humanity, I take three main planets, namely

Uranus, Jupiter and Saturn. Uranus signifies technology, revolution and evolution. No Uranus, no Aquarian age. Uranus, therefore, is the main significator of the Aquarian age. It might amaze readers to know that in astronomy, Jupiter is the heavyweight of the zodiac. It has great magnetism. Jupiter attracts planets to itself so that they may not go to the Sun and combust. Therefore, by astronomy, Jupiter is also the protector of the planets. The same is true of Jupiter and astrology. In 2020, Jupiter and Saturn will clasp the hands of each other and therefore Jupiter (protection) and Saturn (stability) will be much more than at other times. But the real pivot, the turning point of our entire existence will be from 20 December 2020 to end of December 2021. I am not a scientist. Instead of 2021 it could extend to 2022. But whatever intuition, imagination, experience of sixty-five years and Ganesha's grace tell me, it is that between 2020 to December 2021, our future will be cast and made.

## THE FINAL CUT-OFF YEAR IS 2080

There is another side to the age of Aquarius. It is complete objectivity, experimentation, progress in science and the development of all our capacities of which we are not fully aware, including neurology, which will come to the fore. Therefore, we live in the most exciting century in the history of mankind. In the words of William Faulkner, the Nobel Prize winner, 'We will not only survive but prevail.' Now I am using all my mental faculties, my great compassion for humanity, the grace of my Lord and Master Ganesha, the force and power of Nature and the galaxies, the cosmos, to say that rightly or wrongly, in 2080, latest space travel will be common and we will be able to use gravity, magnetic forces, our own life force and also other forces, which we are not aware of right now, for the union, use and joy of technology and humanity. On Tuesday, the day of Ganesha, I say very humbly that this is my last word.

# Achievements

## BEJAN DARUWALLA

Bejan was invited to the wedding ceremony of Kapil Sharma, the well-known comedian. Bejan had predicted his success. The CNBC, Zee Business and ANI where invited and Bejan told them categorically that Modi will win the game and scatter the Opposition to the four corners of the world.

Just for the record we state that Bejan was acknowledged as one of the hundred great astrologers in the last thousand years in the great *Millenium Book of Prophecy*, published by HarperCollins, USA.

He was awarded the highest degree of Vedic astrology, 'Jyotishi Mahamahopadhaya', by the Federation of Indian Astrologers.

He was the astrologer in residence at the Manila Hotel, Philippines.

Bejan featured on the BBC, in Hard Talk India, August 1999. Bejan was born on 11 July 1931. He has a family of five, including his wife and three children. He loves them more than his life.

His hobbies are watching cartoons and sports, listening to music, telling jokes, reading books on philosophy and laughing at himself.

Among the supporters and patrons of Bejan he specially mentions Behram Mehta. Behram Mehta is the producer and promoter of the internationally famous Aava mineral water. It might be interesting to know that Aava is the pious and holy river of the Parsees. Behram was mainly responsible for motivating and inspiring Bejan to write this book because the latter felt washed out. Old supporters and patrons – Lakshyaraj Singh Mewar, City Palace, Udaipur, Neeraj Bajaj and Vikram Singh – deserve Bejan's salute. He acknowledges his love and respect for

Shri Devendra Fadnavis, chief minister of Maharashtra, Shri Bhupendra Chudasma, education minister of Gujarat, Shri Parshottam Rupala, and Shri Vijay Rupani, chief minister of Gujarat, Dadi Mistry and Jimmy Mistry. He is on very happy and cordial terms with them.

Kishore Kumar Kaya, the owner of the ancient hotel Savoy, hosted his entire family in a royal style at Mussoorie. Bejan tried to guide him to the best of his limited ability. He found Kishore and his wife Madhu very religious and charitable. Hotel owners come no better.

Ekta, the beautiful and brilliant leading lady of Radio Mirchi, came to Bejan's place and he recited two poems on our prime minister Narendra Modi. Both of them approved of the idea and the poems.

## NASTUR DARUWALLA

Nastur and his wife, Meetu, went with great pride and honour to pay their respects to the scintillating, peerless Prince Lakshyaraj Singh Mewar of City Palace, Udaipur, and the Royal Princess Nivritti Singh Mewar as the divine royal daughter was born to this royal couple. Prince Lakshyaraj Singh Mewar is like a son to Nastur's father, Bejan Daruwalla, and Bejan says he will bring glory to all.

Nastur clearly predicted in *Amar Ujala*, Lucknow edition, that Chief Minister Yogi Adityanath will defeat the combination of Mayawati and Akhilesh Yadav. It was not easy, but he did it superbly.

In the same paper, he clearly predicted that Shri Narendra Modi Saheb will come back to power and there was no election at all as Narendra Modi Saheb single-handedly took his party to great victory.

Nastur was invited with great love and respect by Shweta Shah from Bhavnagar, who herself is a very good and efficient Reiki master, to inaugurate a centre for different forms of healing and spiritual togetherness by Samarth Vyas. The event was a huge success.

Nastur once again says 'Big God bless you' to Shri Byram Avari Saheb, Avari Group of Hotels, Karachi, and his entire family because seldom such noble people are born and they have made the Parsee community and the world proud by their humanitarian actions.

# Personalities

Ganesha says hats off to Premji for his philanthropy, integrity, ability to create a mighty organization and influencing a generation into wisdom and generosity as well as an exuberance of spirit, adventure and kindness. Both Premji and his counterpart Murthy, of Infosys, are Leos. To me Leo means pure radiance. That says it all.

Under the excuse of 'America First', Donald Trump has proved his negativity, insularity and his combativeness in trade war with China, and Mexico in particular. I admit I could be wrong but he is certainly not the most respected and loved president of America.

Pritish Nandy, a genius, former editor of the *Times of India*, a poet of repute and a man who knows his own mind, and is not afraid to say it, deserves my admiration and praise. I have known him for a thousand years so to say. This Capricorn is both genuine and generous.

I have said a million times that Narendra Modi is the future of our country. I have already said in my 2019 book that BJP will again be in power. There is a poem on him. It says it all.

Anupam Kher, the well-known film actor, producer and director is a Piscean. I have met him thrice and with his brilliance and sheer imaginative sympathy, he does, and will continue to, shine like a star.

Yes, I have met and dined with the Cancerian Gautam Adani along with the famous Virgo spiritualist Sadhguru. I know Gautam Adani is a giant industrialist. But to me it is much more important that he has built a first-class hospital where the poor and needy can find solace and help. Sadhguru is one of the greatest personalities of the world. This is my personal belief.

I have often said that Angela Merkel of Germany – the Cancerian – is perhaps the greatest leader of the world. But I cannot say the same for Libran Vladimir Putin of Russia and Kim Jong-un of North Korea. Shinzo Abe, the Virgo, has my full admiration and praise. Above all, I am convinced that the Dalai Lama, the Cancerian, is sent by God almighty for spreading compassion in the world. I may be right or wrong, but to me compassion and consciousness are twins.

Right now, as I am writing this piece on 7 June 2019, the World Cup is on. Virat Kohli, the Scorpio, is flamboyant and has tucked many runs under his belt. But to me, for whatever it is worth, Taureans Sachin Tendulkar and Brian Lara are slightly superior and I certainly know my cricket. Rohit Sharma is also a Taurean and Bradman, perhaps the greatest cricketer the world has ever produced, is a Virgo. My observation is that the Virgos and Taureans, both earthy signs, make the greatest batsmen. But I admit openly that time could prove me wrong. In other words, a batsman of any sign has the ability to be the greatest ever. In other words, the key to life, cricket and love is to keep an open mind and admit that one could go wrong.

I repeat what I said before, 'In love and in cricket

Even the great Daruwalla can lose his wicket.'

# Modi and India

The Ganges, your mother/the Himalayas, your father/beckon you for a blessing/they say/'the good and the great/are seldom knit/ in the same human/but may you have both/ May your feet of clay/alchemize into tensile steel/ not intelligence, not cleverness, not sharpness,/ but wisdom and an open mind/ will enable you/to do the right thing at the right time and the right place/It is your dharma and your karma/to make India shining clean/from sole to soul/you will help to heal the world and make it whole/ Narendra, this is your real destiny/Fulfil it.'

– BEJAN DARUWALLA, *Spiritual Sizzlers*, HarperCollins (2015)

Ganesha says my devotee Bejan Daruwalla predicted the mighty success of Narendra Modi as early as 29 March 2012 in Kanoria Centre for Arts, Ahmedabad. Bejan said that Modi will tear the Opposition to shreds and then light a fire with them. Terrible words. How true. Actually, he said Modi will do the TFCD (Todi, Fodi, Chiri, Dhoi Nakhse) which is the Gujarati equivalent to the above. Bejan has met Modi twice. Here is a quote from the *Times of India*, 29 May 2019: 'What the country does in the next five years will determine its destiny. All hesitations and frictions characterising our complex bureaucratic system must be overcome and wheels of the economy freed from the mud and sand that keep it from racing to double-digit growth.'

Astrology is all about timing. The secret of Modi's success is that he has the capacity, the intelligence and the ability to think, observe and deliver the goods. Very surprisingly, the sheer personality of Modi and his oratorical skills have a multifold impact on the masses. Personality is the result of all your experiences and magnetic force, which is difficult to define – either you have it, or you do not have it. Yes, I agree that these are plus points, but Modi is a Virgo. Virgo means purity and cleanliness. Therefore, along with all the other good qualities, it is my prediction that Modi is born to cleanse Mother Ganga. I support this statement as Modi was born on 17 September. The Tarot card shows a lady pouring water to nourish the earth. The title is 'the star'. To me, Mother Ganga is divinity. When I met him, he asked me only question: 'Will our India be great?' Just as human beings have their birthdate, countries also have their birthdate. By Western mundane astrology, India certainly comes under the sign Capricorn. Jupiter, the planet of plenty and prosperity, will be in the sign Capricorn from 2 December 2019 to 18 December 2020. Jupiter will join hands with Saturn (responsibility, religion and duty), which is also in Capricorn. Therefore, this extremely powerful double thrust will push, drive and motivate our country to great success. It is a magnetic turbo for India. I know very well that results take time. India is multicultural, plural and has many tongues, traditions, customs, rituals, ceremonies and all the religions of the world; and we Indians have the freedom to express our own opinion and ideas. It is the way democracy works. Yes, it takes time to deliver the complete results. Therefore, the predictions of this Ganesha devotee is that from 2020 to 2026, India will attain the status of a superpower. More importantly, India will help to make the world united, happy and peaceful.

The astrologer is mainly a visionary. I use Indian astrology, Western astrology, the Tarot card, palm reading, runes and my own invention of the dice. Above all, I pray to Mother Nature and Mother Ganga and say very humbly that I am not a god, but I try my best with my limited ability, and leave the rest to cosmic forces. Though a former professor of English, I have no desire to lecture and preach. I only say may the life force be with all of us.

(Written on 29 May 2019)

## AMIT SHAH AND MODI

Ganesha says Amit Shah and Modi make a powerful team together. Why? Amit Shah was born on the twenty-second day of a month. 2 + 2 = 4. Modi was born on the seventeenth. 1 + 7 = 8. Four is half of eight and India's ruling number is 8, example 26 January, our Republic Day, i.e., 2 + 6 = 8. Also, Amit Shah's Jupiter is in the sign Taurus, an earthy sign. Normally, Jupiter in Taurus makes slightly plumb. Modi's sign is Virgo also an earthy sign. Therefore, a beautiful and complete match. Usually, I do not go into the technicalities of astrology and numerology. But here I make a difference.

The million-dollar question is: Can Amit Shah do for India what he has done for the BJP? My answer is yes. The main reason for it is that Amit Shah combines organizing ability, a certain degree of tolerance, the vision to see ahead for the good of all and, above all, the Libra charm of persuasion and the Scorpio instinct for investigation and probing when he gets into the heart of things. This is the master key to his success.

In a telephonic conversation, Amit Shah told me that his favourite colour is pink. Pink is a combination of red and white. Red stands for Mars. Mars means energy, investigation and results. White stands for Sun. Sun means politics, limelight, publicity and prominence. This fits the bill for Amit Shah.

The real time for delivering the goods for our country is the next year itself. The next year decides the fate of India for the whole of the remaining twenty-first century. I know very well that this is a bold statement. But I have eighty-eight years in my pocket. My Lord and Master is Ganesha and, while not a god, I work very hard in my profession and I believe I have the vision, though it might be incomplete, to look into the future. I call upon the cosmic force of the universe and respect all religions. The years 2022 and 2023 will very possibly be the finest ones for our country. India could well be the superpower. I say this very humbly because I am not a god.

# In Memorium

I miss my guru, Vashisht Mehta, very much. I remember his key word. Astrology is the art of synthesis. Synthesis means the art of putting everything together in the right place at the right time.

Malay, the son of my mighty good friend the late Gautam Vimal Shah, met his end in May 2019.

It was a double blow to me. Whatever people may say about death, I openly admit that it shakes me up completely and I do not reconcile myself completely to it. That's the way with it.

# Astro-analysis of Terrorists and Suicide Bombers

Ganesha says it is time to go digital and explain about the terrorist and suicide bomber in this way: Mars (violence, confidence, powerful determination to accomplish the objective; energy put into action) + Mercury (superb communication and secrecy and deceit and camouflage of real purpose) + Sun (need for prestige, power, position) + Uranus (the actual making of the bomb. Pluto is associated deeply with the atomic bomb itself) + Saturn (attention only on target. Not caring for the results on others and the sufferings it will cause).

Pluto is power plus.

I am not going to give lectures about the suicide bombers and the terrorists. But in the words of Webster, the horror and impact of the heinous actions of the terrorists can be summed up as 'horror piled upon horror'. Devastation of entire families moves me tremendously. But by 2020–21, the terrorists will be completely nabbed, imprisoned and out of action.

But this is my last word. The terrorists and the suicide bombers show us a horrible waste of life which could be used for better purposes as the terrorists and the suicide bombers could have had many good things going for them and for others. This is the tragedy.

# ESP and Astrology

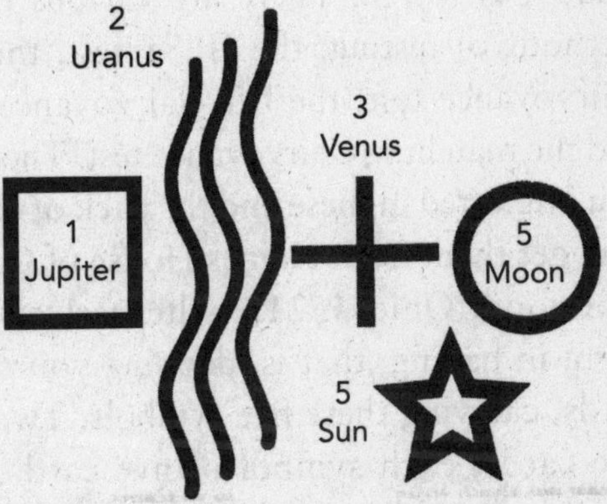


Take a good look at these symbols. We are going to test your ESP (extrasensory perception) by them. Later, we are going to blend it with astrology. The symbols are actually cards designed at the Parapsychology Laboratory (Duke University, USA) to test ESP. ESP is the faculty of seeing mentally what is happening or existing out of sight.

You can call it intuition, or the sixth sense.

Yes, I have converted these symbols into planets and astrology with my experience and imagination and research. I do not claim it as final. But I am presenting it to you for what it is worth. There are various other methods of testing: the GEST test, the BT clairvoyance test, the DT clairvoyance test and the matching clairvoyance test. Those of you interested in these and the pack of cards, may get them from Haines House of Cards, Norwood, Ohio 45212. Alternatively, no harm in having, that is, devising your own cards, carrying these five symbols. Twenty-five cards, each symbol of five cards, are enough. Should you feel like probing further into the mysteries of the ESP card, please read *Parapsychology, Frontier Science of the Mind*, by J.B. Rhine and J.G.Pratt (Charles C. Thomas, 1957).

Generally, those who select the Star as the first preference are ambitious and dominating. If you like the Cross best, accept sensuality, as well as sacrifice, as part of your make-up. If the Circle be your first love, it shows spiritual tendencies, a hypersensitive nature, wild imagination and a streak of femininity even in the males (nothing wrong in it, if you ask me, as most poets have feminine souls!). Those who love the Wavy Lines, will do splendidly in the arts as well as the sciences but not commerce. If the Square is your first love, you'll be lucky, find protection and money, and never remain poor.

The third card you choose is the balance wheel of your personality. Often, it shows what helps you from going off your mind. By my findings, the Sun gives results in your first, tenth, nineteenth, twenty-eighth, thirty-seventh, forty-sixth, fifty-fifth, sixty-fourth, seventy-third, eighty-second and ninety-first year. Venus around your sixth, fifteenth, twenty-fourth, thirty-third, forty-second, fifty-first, sixtieth, sixty-ninth, seventy-eighth, eighty-seventh, ninety-sixth. The Moon around your second, eleventh, twentieth, twenty-ninth, thirty-eighth, forty-seventh, fifty-sixth, sixty-fifth, seventy-fourth, eighty-third, ninety-second. Jupiter around your third, twelfth, twenty-first, thirtieth, thiry-ninth, forty-eighth, fifty-seventh, sixty-sixth, seventy-fifth, eighty-fourth, ninety-third. Uranus around your fourth, thirteenth, twenty-second, thirty-first, fortieth, forty-ninth, fifty-eighth, sixty-seventh, seventy-sixth, eighty-fifth, ninty-fourth.

I have always applied Western astrology to Vedic mantras. That has given me excellent results. If you like the Square, the main planet is Jupiter for it and the mantra is '*Om Jhram Jhreem Jhroom Sa Gurave Namah*'.

It would be interesting for the readers to note that by astronomy, Jupiter is the heavyweight of the zodiac and attracts other planets to it, so that the other planets do not go to the Sun and get totally combusted. To me, personally, Jupiter is the saviour of humanity. The other mantra is for the Sun: '*Om Hram Hreem Hrom Sa Suryaya Namah*'.

I do not know why but I do not take the other mantras into consideration for the other planets. I can only say that this is the way I am made. Finally, one can combine it with the horoscope, as I do, or use this method by itself. It is exciting, informative, but not infallible. Nothing ever is!

# Cartoons and Comedy (Effect of Mercury)

Ganesha says cartoons and comedy are the finest ways to relax, have fun and laugh away to glory. Why? In cartoons, normally, nobody dies. You can fall from a mountain, fight, love, leap, dance and be larger than life itself. Normally people identify with the cartoons and therefore they can be larger than life and be whatever they want. It is a sort of wish-fulfilment. One does not need astrology to understand this but just for your information, Mercury, the planet of communication, contacts and versatility (ability) is the chief planet for it. Taking an example from sports even, cricket and tennis very specially come under the impact of Mercury. Why tennis? Mercury refers very specially to the arms and in tennis service, volleys, backhand and forehand are most important. Finally, let me say that Mercury juggles the neurological nervous system in the brain. Mercury has much to do with a sharp and brilliant brain.

# Ramana Maharshi's Truth

There is neither creation
nor destruction,
neither destiny
nor free will;
neither path
nor achievement.
This is the final truth.

– RAMANA MAHARSHI

Something in my genes, blood, bones, the subconscious, the mind, the heart and the soul responds instinctively to this saying of Ramana Maharshi. Maybe it is being an Indian and an astrologer that makes me zero in. This I *feel*. If anybody knows what truth is, it is the great seer and sage Ramana Maharshi.

# Your Bonus for 2020

## KNOW YOUR JUPITER

Whatever defect I have – of eye, of heart, of mind, or whatever excess there is – may Brihaspati (Jupiter) remedy it. Gracious to us be the Lord of the world.

– YAJUR VEDA 36.2

Yes, Jupiter in Indian astrology is best known as the 'Lord of the world'. Ganesha has enlightened me with this unique combination of Jupiter and the Vedic hymn:

Many are the gifts of His Spirit,
His blessings – never exhausted,
For He showers His worshippers
with fullness of knowledge and light.

Jupiter has a big-bellied body with a broad, prominent chest and a voice like a lion. His body, hair and eyes are of a tawny hue that shines like pure gold. Predominantly *kapha* in constitution and fond of sweets, he wears yellow clothes and yellow flowers. The Brahmana Jupiter knows the Vedas and is an expert in all forms of knowledge. He possesses all virtues and is modest, forgiving and happy. His mind and senses are disciplined and his intellect subtle. Attached to ritual, he follows the path of righteousness. His metal is gold and gem topaz.

Lord of the body's fat, of the north-east, of Thursday, and of the constellations Sagittarius and Pisces, Jupiter is known as the Lord of worship and the guru. His titles are teacher of the immortals, the soul, the advisor, the lord of speech, the golden, the creator, the irresistible, he who wears yellow, the young, the worthy of worship throughout the world, the compassionate, creator of polity, remover of oppression, and the peaceable.

Dear readers, I have given you an excellent image of Jupiter as seen in Vedic Indian astrology! Now let me elucidate the uses, benefits and influences of Jupiter in simple and plain language so that you get the most mileage of megabytes:

1. Essentially, it is the planet of good luck, or the greater fortune.
2. Jupiter stands for joviality, earlier called as love.
3. It is the planet of the three Ws, namely, wealth and wisdom and worship, and obviously that's saying a great deal.
4. Jupiter signifies a robust and even rumbustious and boisterous attitude to life. In other words, Jupiter is both cheerful and noisy.
5. This is the planet of expansion – that means weight problems, sincerity, the readiness and ability

to learn as well as teach, a truly grand vision of life, easy access to money, popularity, power, position, prosperity, the four Ps that I like to use.

6. Comforts and luxuries fall under the bracket of both Jupiter and Venus. Vehicles and pomp and flair for doing things with savoir faire also come in the ambit of Jupiter and Venus.
7. Jupiter is wise and generous, whereas Mercury is clever and shrewd.
8. Jupiter is friendly and good for practically everything: you can deal with bankers, influential people, get a job, start long journeys, begin religious ceremonies and rites.
9. Jupiter refers to charities, gold, honey, cows, chariots, elder brother, the north-east direction;

and among body parts and organs – tantra and mantra, right conduct, yellow topaz; and among body parts and organs – liver, gall bladder, pancreas, spleen, fat, blood arteries, thighs, ear, sense of smell; and among afflictions – anaemia and laziness. Colours will be royal purple, yellow, indigo and red in combination. Jupiter also stands for treasures, wealth and ancient language. His day is Thursday, and his flower, the chrysanthemum.

10. Many astrologers also take tin as the metal of Jupiter and turquoise as the gem. Personally, I take the number 3 and its series, 21=2+1 =3, 12=1+2=3, as the lucky number of Jupiter. Many a time, Jupiter in your horoscope speaks of remarkable organizing ability and managerial excellence.

11. In short, Jupiter is the bestower of goodies; call him Santa Claus if you will.

## MIGHTY ASTRONOMICAL FACT ABOUT JUPITER

Jupiter helps you, both by astrology and astronomy. By astronomy Jupiter is the saviour of the planets because it attracts all the planets. If it does not do so, the other planets will go towards the Sun, which will burn them all out of existence. Therefore, by astrology and by astronomy, Jupiter is the saviour of our universe.

## JUPITER IN CAPRICORN FROM 2 DECEMBER 2019 TO 18 DECEMBER 2020

Walt Disney, the king of cartoons, Charlie Chaplin, the ultimate cinema comedian, Danny Kaye, another giant of comedy, all had Jupiter in Capricorn in their sun signs. Why? Capricorn is a solid, steady, stable sign. But Jupiter is lively, cheerful, as bouncy as a tennis ball. Jupiter enjoys both love and laughter as I said at the outset. Therefore, the comic aspect of Jupiter in Capricorn is strongly reflected.

At the other and of the scale we have Adolf Hilter, Richard Nixon and Robert F. Kennedy, with Jupiter in Capricorn. All three were in their own way powerful leaders. Hitler was an evil genius. Nixon was charged for impeached. Kennedy had numerous love affairs, ruffled the feathers of many people, and was finally shot dead. In other words, all three, though, totally different in mental make-up and the use of power, came to a very sorry and tragic end. The power and the tragic end were both because of the sign Capricorn. The charm and magnetism were the influence of Jupiter. Ganesha says this is the wide range of Jupiter in Capricorn.

Your best luck comes to you through your industry and ambition. While you will do well in almost any career you choose to follow, you are particularly fortunate in occupations that have to do with politics, cinema, entertainment, business, leadership, empire building, industry, real estate, construction, geology, mining, farming, financing. In other words, you have many options.

You can be generous and tight-fisted at the same time, reach the topmost position of excellence, work hard and be the perfect taskmaster. You will always have strong likes and dislikes.

In personal relationships, goals, status, sense of purpose and social climbing, integrity and honesty will be very important, as important as love itself. In other words, in a relationship you will work hard and long for both material success and real joy which comes from sincere efforts. I do not have Jupiter in Capricorn. But I do endorse the tremendous effort and sacrifice those with Jupiter in Capricorn make. Hats off to them!

## JUPITER IN AQUARIUS FROM 19 DECEMBER 2020 TO 28 DECEMBER 2021 (ROUGHLY)

Ganesha says with Jupiter in Aquarius the modern age of science and technology will be at full speed for the remaining year. Albert Einstein, the man of the millennium, the father of modern science, had Jupiter in Aquarius. Why? Aquarius is the sign of the New Age, the millennium, the modern times, the twenty-first century, and Jupiter is the planet of both knowledge and wisdom. Therefore, Jupiter in Aquarius leads to inventions, research, new methods and modes which improve the quality of life. It speaks of television, computers, electronics, aviation and the space industry. So powerful is this New Age influence that I am making an exception and quoting at length.

> You have strong intuitions and original ideas, and you like to cultivate your mind. You do not value money for its own sake, but for what it can do to satisfy the material

> needs of others. You are a humanitarian first and foremost. Purely commercial ventures bore you. You make excellent scientists, doctors, lawyers, architects, investors, bankers, ambassadors and statesmen. You would do well as teachers, speakers, scientists, labour leaders and psychologists. You may also be fortunate in the many fields of entertainment, and particularly in music. You are likely to be active in charitable or social work, and you can excel in jobs connected with transportation by air. Often, also, your best opportunities lie in government or other big organizations, or where it is an advantage to be popular with the masses.
>
> – Joan Quigley

The numbers 3, 4, 8 often play an important part in your life. The colours blue and aquamarine (and the stone) will be lucky for you.

In relationship you will realize your ideals and hopes and they will come from sharing. Yes, you will make lasting friendships and marriage should be good for you. It will also be an enduring relationship. Ganesha says you will think positively and that will lead to happiness. The best part is you will stimulate your friend, mate, partner, associate, and all those who come in direct contact with you. You will be an evolved human being. That's saying everything.

## FOR READERS

It is quite possible that you may find my view of your own placing of Jupiter not perfect and sometimes not totally applicable to you. The reason is that Jupiter in any sign is not the only placing. We also have Saturn, Mercury, Venus, Sun, Moon, Pluto, Neptune and Uranus in any of the twelve signs. All of these have an influence and therefore an impact on your horoscope. Therefore, no one planet in one sign can be truly enough, or representative of your total personality and complete character. This is what makes the horoscope so fascinating and difficult to read and interpret.

# Bejan Opens Out

Ganesha devotee Bejan Daruwalla is writing this piece on 8 June 2019 as the World Cup is on. Just as in the World Cup there are opening batsmen, Bejan also open the innings of his life and his heart. Bejan says one never asks a painter what he paints. The simple reason is that the whole world is the canvas of the painter. In the same way, not only the world but the cosmos is the area of the astrologer. We are a box of assorted chocolates. Twelve signs, therefore, at least twelve different people. The one problem which has beaten me is that we have everything going for us and yet we continue to fight, squabble and make ourselves miserable and unhappy. This has been going on since time immemorial. I agree there have been prophets, leaders, peacemakers and visionaries who have stepped in from time to time to ease our pain and often make us happy. But it is for a short time.

Now, to me the twenty-first century is the biggest, best and brightest in the history of mankind. Mankind is getting into artificial intelligence, genes, microbiology, the sheer abundance and variety of Mother Nature, modern amenities, the neurological power and possibility of our brain which we are now learning to use completely, a chance to do away with sickness and disease and improve our own way of life and thinking, adjustment and even mitigation climate change and, above all, creation of a new efficiency for ourselves and the world. We human beings are of the Earth, but we can not only reach out to the stars but actually go there and create a brand-new world. To put it simply we have a chance to be happy in every possible way. We just need to be tolerant and scientifically minded, to accept the changes of the world and yet be our own natural selves. I know it is very easy to say this and mighty difficult to put it into practice. But we human beings can adapt and adopt to each given situation. We are truly masters of resilience. Therefore, taking all of this into consideration, I say with conviction and courage that happiness and well-being is our rightful inheritance and legacy. Three cheers! Many scientists believe God will not be necessary after 100 years. They are welcome to their opinion. I can only say that according to the Upanishads, the nature of consciousness could very well lead us to the final truth of the entire cosmos. That is my final word.

# Mantras

Ganesha says we Indians believe in the power, myth, light and vibrations of mantras. Therefore, I am giving a few mantras.

The mantra for Sun is: '*Om Hram Hreem Hrom Sa Suryaya Namah*'.

The mantra for Mars is: '*Om Kraam Kreem Krom Sa Bhowmaya Namah*'.

The mantra for Mercury is: '*Om Bram Breem Browm Sa Budhaya Namah*'.

The mantra for Jupiter is: '*Om Jhram Jhreem Jhroom Sa Gurave Namah*'.

The mantra for Saturn is: '*Om Praam Preem Proum Sa Sanaye Namah*'.

The mantra for Rahu is: '*Om Bhram Bhreem Bhroum Sa Rahave Namah*'.

The mantra for Ketu is: '*Om Praam Preem Proum Sa Kethave Namah*'.

# About the Authors

## BEJAN DARUWALLA

Ganesha says that though it may be true that Bejan Daruwalla is one of the 100 great astrologers in the last 1,000 years, he is perhaps the only one who has read the fortune of three prime ministers of India, namely, Morarji Desai, Atal Bihari Vajpayee and Narendra Modi. This Ganesha devotee at eighty-eight believes that goodness and compassion are much more important and certainly universal. He now believes in keeping a very low profile and tries to bless all people sincerely and with all the limited power that he has. In other words, in the wide, wide world, there is no substitute for sheer goodness. Goodness (including integrity) matters a million times more than greatness is Ganesha devotee Bejan's final word.

## NASTUR DARUWALLA

How can I ever forget the scintillating prince, Lakshyaraj Singh of Mewar City Palace, Udaipur, who is like a son to me, as he has the divine blessings of Lord Ekling-ji of Shakti Peeth as the temple belongs to his great royal ancestors. If you have Lord Shiva with you what is more to say. My son Nastur stays in the heart of Prince Lakshyaraj Singh who is always ready to help the needy and downtrodden in life.

My son got blessings from the top industrialist of India, Shri Neeraj R. Bajaj, son of my patron Ramkrishna Bajaj for progress in life. I call Neeraj Bajaj my divine son as our relationship is at least fifty years old.

The coming back to power of the chief minister of Gujarat, Shri Vijay Rupani, was the bold and correct prediction of my son when all others were thinking that the chief minister will be changed. My son again got encouragement and blessings for progress in life and for writing this book from the education minister of Gujarat, Shri Bhupendrasinh Chudasma.

My another beloved son and top industrialist of Mumbai, Shri Jimmey Mistry, gave his good wishes so that my legacy can continue in the form of my son Nastur.

# Contact Information

**WhatsApp/Call**

+91 8141234275

**Email**

info@bejandaruwalla.com

**Website**

www.bejandaruwalla.com